W0050222

SET THEORY

FOR SMARTYPANTS

Anushka Ravishankar

ILLUSTRATED BY
Pia Alizé Hazarika

duckbill

An imprint of Penguin Random House

DUCKBILL BOOKS

USA | Canada | UK | Ireland | Australia
New Zealand | India | South Africa | China | Singapore

Duckbill Books is part of the Penguin Random House group of companies
whose addresses can be found at global.penguinrandomhouse.com

Published by Penguin Random House India Pvt. Ltd
4th Floor, Capital Tower 1, MG Road,
Gurugram 122 002, Haryana, India

Penguin
Random House
India

First published in Duckbill Books by
Penguin Random House India 2024

Text copyright © Anushka Ravishankar 2024
Illustrations copyright © Pia Alizé Hazarika 2024

All rights reserved

10 9 8 7 6 5 4 3 2 1

This is a work of non-fiction. The views and opinions expressed in this book are the
author's own and the facts are as reported by her which have been verified to the extent
possible, and the publishers are not in any way liable for the same.

ISBN 9780143461043

Typeset in ArcherPro by DiTech Publishing Services Pvt. Ltd
Printed at Thomson Press India Ltd, New Delhi

This book is sold subject to the condition that it shall not, by way of trade
or otherwise, be lent, resold, hired out, or otherwise circulated without the
publisher's prior consent in any form of binding or cover other than that in
which it is published and without a similar condition including this condition
being imposed on the subsequent purchaser.

www.penguin.co.in

SET THEORY is the mathematical theory of well-defined collections—called sets— which comprise of distinct objects that are called **members** or **elements** of the set.

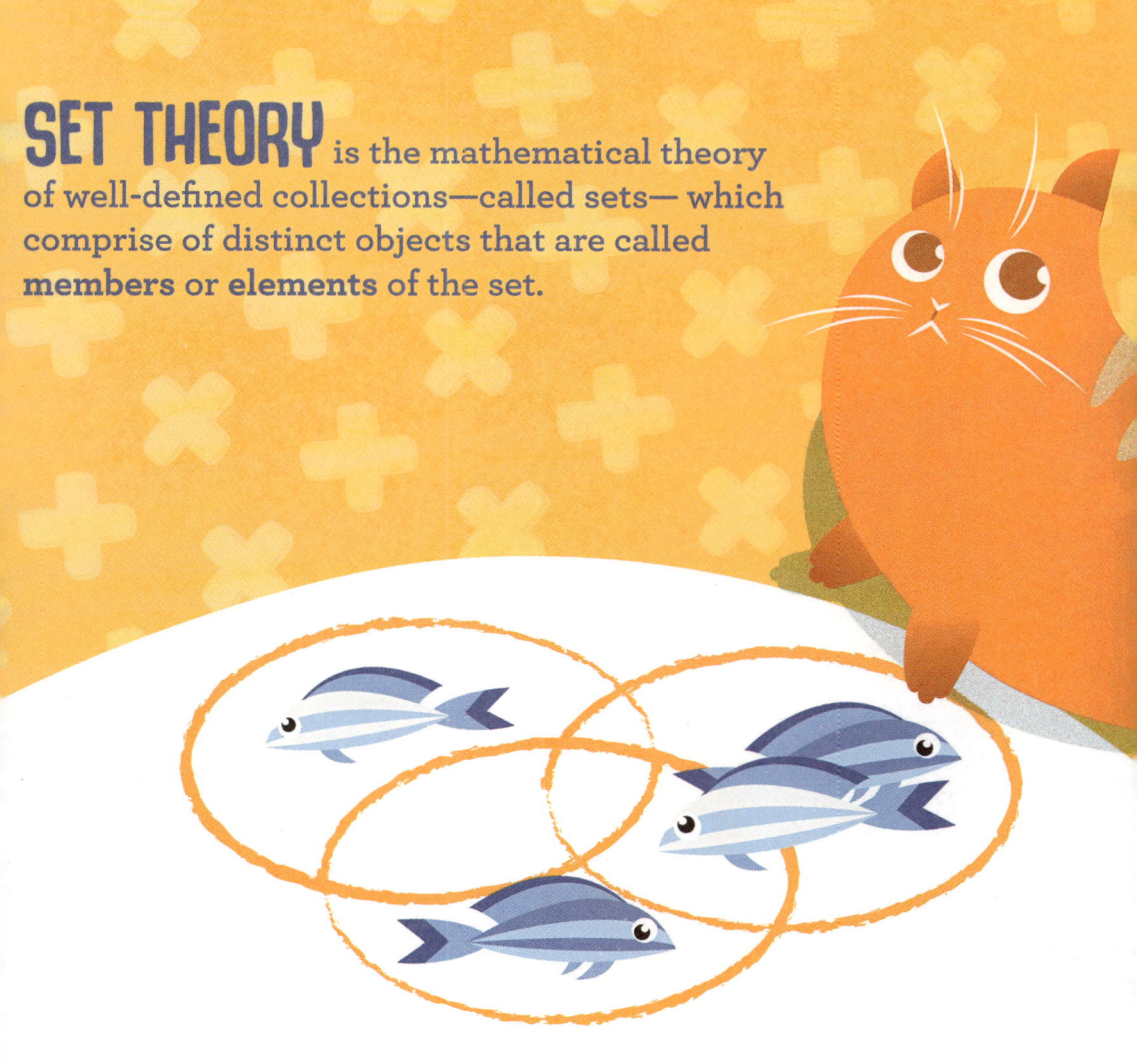

A **set** is a collection of objects or things.
These objects could be anything: numbers,
letters, hairpins, dogs, people . . .

Like the set of all cats. Or the set of all fish.

The object in a set is called an **element** of that set. So if we have a set of all cats, for example, every cat in the world is an element of that set.

The elements of a set don't have to be related.

You can have a bicycle and a banana in a set.
You can have a cat and a dog in a set.

$\{ 1\ _2\ ^3\ _4\ ^5 \}$

A set is shown with a pair of squiggly brackets, one on each side.

{1, 2, 3, 4, 5} is the set of numbers from 1 to 5.

{apple, mango, banana, pear, papaya} is a set of five fruits.

A set can have anything in it.

A set need not contain only real things. It can be made up of anything that you can imagine.

It can even have things that cannot be imagined.

So a set of all things that cannot be imagined is a set too!

Some sets are **finite**. This means they have a fixed number of elements that can be counted.

The set of letters in the word 'cat' is a finite set because we can count the number of letters: {c, a, t}

The set of children in one classroom is a finite set because we can count the number of children.

Some sets are **infinite**. This means that they have an endless number of elements.

The set of all the grains of sand on a beach is an infinite set because you cannot count them.

The set of all numbers is an infinite set because though they can be counted, all the numbers cannot be listed.

Sometimes, a set can also have nothing in it. This is called a **null set**.

For example, the set of all cats that bark is a null set. BARKING CATS = {}

A **Venn diagram** is used to show a set visually.

Let's say you have a set called CATS, which is made up of seven cats:
CATS = {Lotto, Pirate, Ziggy, Eecha, Pintu, Chintu, Ickle, Smartypants}

This means that the set CATS is made up of these eight elements.

CATS

CHINTU

ZIGGY

LOTTO

SMARTYPANTS

PIRATE

EECHA

ICKLE

PINTU

Venn diagrams can be used to show the
relationships between sets.

Ziggy, Lotto, Eecha and Chintu like to eat tuna.
TUNA = {Ziggy, Lotto, Eecha, Chintu}

Smartypants, Eecha and Lotto like mackerel.
MACKEREL = {Smartypants, Lotto, Eecha}

So now we know all the cats who like either tuna *or* mackerel.

The set of CATS WHO LIKE EITHER TUNA OR MACKEREL is made up of all the elements in TUNA and all the elements in MACKEREL.

This set can be shown like this:
{Ziggy, Lotto, Eecha, Chintu, Smartypants}

This is how we can show the set of cats who like either tuna *or* mackerel in a Venn diagram.

This is called the **Union** of the sets TUNA and MACKEREL, and is shown with the symbol U.

TUNA U MACKEREL = {Ziggy, Lotto, Eecha, Chintu, Smartypants}

TUNA AND MACKEREL

The Venn diagram also shows us which cats like tuna *and* mackerel. The cats that like both tuna and mackerel are part of both the circles.

The area which is part of both the circles is called the **Intersection** of the sets TUNA and MACKEREL. It is shown with an upside down ∪ like this: ∩.

TUNA ∩ MACKEREL = {Lotto, Eecha}

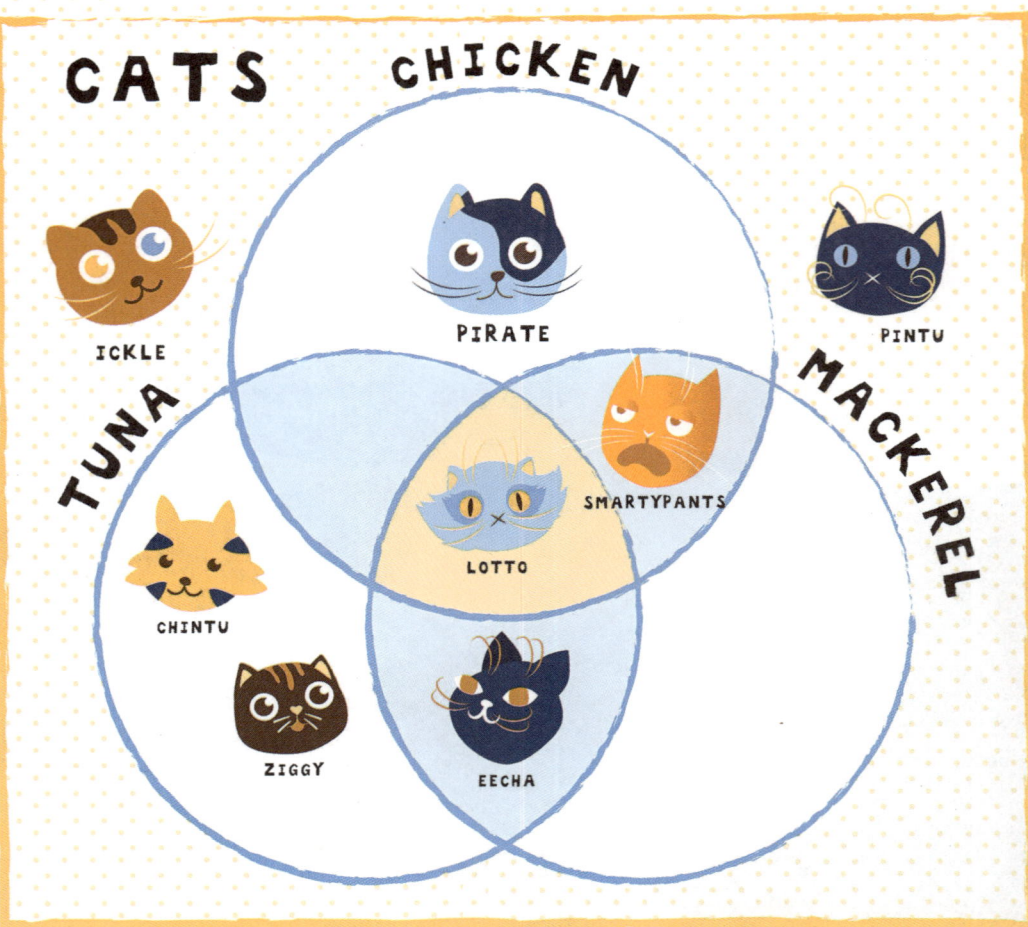

CATS CHICKEN

ICKLE

PIRATE

PINTU

TUNA

MACKEREL

CHINTU

SMARTYPANTS

LOTTO

ZIGGY

EECHA

Let's now make a set of the cats who like chicken.

CHICKEN = {Smartypants, Lotto, Pirate}

All the elements of the three sets, CHICKEN, TUNA and MACKEREL, are also in the set CATS.

Ickle and Pintu don't like chicken, tuna or mackerel, so they are part of the set CATS but not part of any of the other sets.

When all the elements of one set are also in another set, then the first set is the **subset** of the second one. It is shown with the symbol ⊆.

So:
CHICKEN ⊆ CATS
TUNA ⊆ CATS
MACKEREL ⊆ CATS

An element **belongs** to a set.

It is shown like this:
Smartypants ∈ CATS

symbol = is the smartest of all
Smartypants ♉ CATS
LIKES ∩ DISLIKES =
{} (NULL SET)
NO TUNA ALLOWED!
OKAY SMARTYPANTS, VERY CLEVER.
YOU KNOW ALL ABOUT SET THEORY NOW.

Anushka Ravishankar likes science, cats and books, not necessarily in that order. So she decided to write a book to explain science to a cat. The cat doesn't always get the point, but she hopes her readers will.

Pia Alizé Hazarika is an illustrator primarily interested in comics and visual narratives.

Her independent/collaborative work has been published by Penguin Random House India (*The PAO Anthology*), Comix India, Manta Ray Comics, The Pulpocracy, Captain Bijli Comics, Yoda Press, Zubaan Books and the Khoj Artists Collective. She runs PIG Studio, an illustration-driven space, based out of New Delhi.

Her handle on Instagram is @_pigstudio_

Read more in the series